THE CHINESE WET MARKET HANDBOOK

PAM SHOOKMAN

BLACKSMITH BOOKS

The Chinese Wet Market Handbook

ISBN 978-988-13764-0-4

Previously published under the title *Roots, Fruits, Shoots and Leaves*

Published by Blacksmith Books
5th Floor, 24 Hollywood Road, Hong Kong
Tel: (+852) 2877 7899
www.blacksmithbooks.com

CONTENTS

INTRODUCTION

Few places capture Hong Kong better than a fresh food market: the cacophony as vendors hawk their goods; the wafting aromas of ripe fruit, dried seafood and medicinal plants; the bright colours of the *gai lan* perfectly arranged in a bamboo basket; and the bustling pace of shoppers elbowing their way to a bargain. These markets provide one of the best ways to get a sense of how Hong Kong people live their lives.

The local way of food shopping is to visit the market every day, buying only what you need for the day's meals. This means that every day you are eating the freshest and healthiest produce possible instead of those droopy leaves lurking at the back of your refrigerator. The liveliest time of day to visit a market is in the morning when the produce is at its perkiest but there's often a second surge around 6pm when people stop at the market on their way home from work.

Hong Kong's food markets are traditionally called wet markets, referring to the regular hosing down of the floors to keep them clean. These days the only part of the market that is bound to be wet is the seafood area.

There are many good reasons for buying food at fresh food markets. Prices are often significantly lower than in supermarkets and the quality is high. You will find a wider variety: not just bananas but banana flowers; not just dragon fruit but dragon fruit flowers (also called hegemony flowers). And the produce is seasonal so what's available in the spring differs greatly from what's available in the fall, a reminder that we needn't pay a fortune for produce that's been picked before it is ripe and shipped in refrigerated containers. When you follow the season you can buy produce when it is at its peak of flavour and nutritional value at a reasonable price.

Seasonality is important. Most people make seasonal adjustments to their clothing and the same should hold for food. By shifting your eating habits to whatever is in season, your tastebuds won't get bored and, according to Chinese medicine, you will be feeding your body what it needs to keep in tip-top shape throughout that season. Chinese medicine classifies foods as heating, cooling or neutral. During Hong Kong's hot and humid summers it is best to eat cooling foods (such as watermelon, daikon and cucumber) whereas during the albeit mild winter your body needs heating foods (such as chilli, chives, walnuts and onions).

The environmental reasons for shopping at local food markets are also compelling. Because most (but by no means all) of what is sold at these markets is produced within the region, the food involves fewer food miles. You are also eliminating the packaging which most supermarket foods are sold in and which causes the produce to sweat and begin to deteriorate.

History lurks in the stands of food markets. Many of the fruits and vegetables listed in these pages are immigrants to Hong Kong. Cashew apples, dragon fruit, custard apples, sweet potatoes and Buddha's hand gourd, for example, arrived from South and Central America via Portuguese and Spanish sailing fleets. This serves as a reminder that the globalisation of food has been occurring for centuries and that the roots of what are considered 'traditional' foods are not as simple as one might think.

This guide is meant to make shopping at a Hong Kong fresh food market easy whether you are a Hong Kong resident who lacks the linguistic and culinary know-how or a tourist who wants to explore Hong Kong's culinary sights. With the guide in hand you will be able to identify foods by their photos, determine how foods are sold through the explanations of the Chinese character signage and locate some of Hong Kong's liveliest food markets with the detailed directions that are given.

The list of foods in the guide is not exhaustive but rather includes those commonly found in Hong Kong's food markets. Some foods go by multiple names so an additional name is included in those cases. Foods commonly found in other parts of the world, such as apples and bananas, are included in a vocabulary list without photos. Some foods, such as cucumber and pumpkin, are featured in the section with photos because they look different than in other parts of the world.

I hope this guide helps you to discover what is available and to have the same pleasure I have had in finding new foods to enjoy eating. Happy shopping!

Pam Shookman

FRUIT

水果

seoi2 gwo2

CASHEW APPLE

(also called Wax Apple and Java Apple)
tin1 tou4

天桃

also called lin4 mou6 蓮霧
Season: May to August
How to eat: Cut into pieces

CENTURY PEAR

seoi2 zing1 lei4

水晶梨

Season: September to December
How to eat: Peel and remove core

CUSTARD APPLE

faan1 gwai2 lai6 zi1

番鬼荔枝

Season: May to August
How to eat: Gently pull off outer skin, cut into wedges and eat around the seeds

DRAGON FRUIT

fo2 lung4 gwo2

火龍果

Season: May to August
How to eat: Pull away the skin and slice

DUCK PEAR
aap3 lei4

鴨梨

Season: September to January
How to eat: Peel and remove core

DURIAN
lao4 lin4

榴槤

also called gam1 zam2 tau4 金枕頭
Season: May to August
How to eat: Saw open and remove the soft flesh inside

FRAGRANT PEAR
hoeng1 lei4

香梨

Season: November to April
How to eat: Peel and remove core

GOOSEBERRY
cou3 leot6

醋栗

Season: June to August
How to eat: Eat whole

GUAVA
faan1 sek6 lau4

番石榴

Season: April to September
How to eat: Peel and slice (optional to
remove the seeds)

HAMI MELON
haa1 mat6 gwaa1

哈蜜瓜

Season: June to September
How to eat: Cut open, remove seeds,
cut away skin and slice

JACKFRUIT
bo1 lo4 mat6

菠蘿蜜

also called daai6 syu6 bo1 lo4 大樹菠蘿
Season: May to September
How to eat: Cut around the middle seed
(jackfruit is usually purchased already
removed from large pod)

KUMQUAT
gam1 gwat1

柑橘

Season: December to March
How to eat: eat whole or cut in half and
discard seeds

LANGSAT
lou4 gu1

蘆菇

Season: June to September
How to eat: Pull off shell and eat the flesh

LONGAN
lung4 ngaan5

龍眼

Season: May to September
How to eat: Pull off shell and eat around central seed

LOQUAT
pei4 paa4

枇杷

also called lou4 gwat1 蘆橘
Season: April to July
How to eat: Peel, cut in half and remove seeds

LYCHEE
lai6 zi1

荔枝

Season: May to August
How to eat: Pull off shell and eat around the central seed

MANGO
mong4 gwo2

芒果

Season: February to August
How to eat: Peel skin and slice away
from the flat seed

MANGOSTEEN
saan1 zuk1

山竹

Season: April to August
How to eat: Pry open skin with a knife
and eat white pods inside

PAPAYA
muk6 gwaa1

木瓜

Season: All year
How to eat: Cut in half lengthwise, scoop out seeds, peel off skin and cut into pieces

PASSION FRUIT
jit6 cing4 gwo2

熱情果

Season: March to June
How to eat: Cut in half and eat the seeds and juicy inside

PEPINO MELON
(also called Tree Melon)
hoeng1 gwaa1 ke4

香瓜茄
Season: January to March
How to eat: Peel and slice (optional to eat the seeds)

PERSIMMON
ci5

柿
also called tim4 ci5 甜柿
or hung4 ci5 紅柿
Season: October to December
How to eat: Pull off top and scoop out the contents with a spoon

POMELO

saa1 tin4 jau6

沙田柚

also called jao6 zi2 柚子
Season: October through December
How to eat: Peel away skin and
membrane

RAMBUTAN

hung4 mou4 daan1

紅毛丹

Season: May to August
How to eat: Pull away the hairy shell,
eat the flesh around the central seed

Red Bayberry
yeung4 mui4

楊梅

Season: May through June
How to eat: Eat around the central seed

Sand Pear
saa1 lei4

沙梨

Season: September to December
How to eat: Peel and core

STAR FRUIT
(also called Carambola)
joeng4 tou4

楊桃
Season: August to February
How to eat: Slice

WAMPEE
wong4pei4

黃皮
Season: June to August
How to eat: Pull off thin skin and eat
around seeds

WATERMELON
sai1 gwaa1

西瓜

Season: May through September
How to eat: Slice into wedges and eat
the red flesh

VEGETABLES

蔬菜

so1 coi3

AMARANTH
jin6 coi3

莧菜

Season: February to July
How to eat: Remove leaves from stem and sauté like spinach

ANGLED LUFFA GOURD
(also called Chinese Okra)
si1 gwaa1

絲瓜

also called sing3 gwaa1 勝瓜
Season: April to October
How to eat: Peel away the ridged edges of the gourd, slice and sauté, stir-fry or pickle

AUBERGINE
(also known as Eggplant)
ke4 gwaa1

茄瓜
also called ai2 gwaa1 矮瓜, ke4 zi2 茄子
Season: All year
How to eat: Slice or cut into chunks and roast, stir-fry or steam

BABY BOK CHOY
baak6 coi3 zai2

白菜仔
Season: All year
How to eat: Steam, braise or slice raw and put in salad

Bamboo Shoots
zuk1 seon2

竹筍

Season: May to September
How to eat: Peel off outer layer, chop and steam or stir-fry; or boil whole, peel and slice for salads

Banana Flower
ziu1 faa1

蕉花

Season: All year
How to eat: Remove the hard outer layers of the flower, slice thinly, soak in lemon water for 5 minutes to prevent colouring, stir-fry or add to salad

BITTER GOURD
fu2 gwaa1

also called loeng4 gwaa1 涼瓜
Season: April to September
How to eat: Cut in half lengthwise,
remove seeds and stir-fry or sauté

BOK CHOY
baak6 coi3

白菜

Season: All year
How to eat: Steam, braise or slice raw
and put in salad

BOX THORN
gau2 gei2 coi3

枸杞菜

Season: December to May
How to eat: Remove leaves from stem
and add to soup

BROAD BEANS
caam4 dau6

蠶豆

also called wu4 dau6 胡豆
or naam4 dau6 南豆
Season: May to June
How to eat: Remove beans from pod
and blanche

BUNASHIMEIJI MUSHROOMS
ling4 zi1 gu1

靈芝菇

Season: All year
How to eat: Trim bottom stem, separate and sauté, stir-fry, braise or add to soup

BURDOCK
ngau4 bong2

牛蒡

Season: July to September
How to eat: Scrape off skin, cut into matchsticks, soak in water for 15 minutes and drain, then stir-fry, simmer or braise

CABBAGE
(also called Napa Cabbage)
wong4 ngaa4 baak6

黃芽白
also called siu6 coi3 紹菜
or daai6 baak6 coi3 大白菜
Season: All year
Slice and stir-fry, braise or add to salads

CALABASH GOURD
(also called Bottle Gourd)
wu4 lou4 gwaa1

葫蘆瓜
Season: May to October
How to eat: Peel, cut in half lengthwise, remove seeds and spongy interior, then slice and sauté, braise or stew

CELTUCE
(also called Stem Lettuce)
wo1 seon2

萵筍
Season: April to October
How to eat: Peel stalk, then slice or
cube it and steam, blanche or stir-fry;
Use leaves in salad

CEYLON SPINACH
(also called Malabar Spinach)
saan4 coi3

潺菜
also called tang4 coi3 藤菜
Season: April to September
How to eat: Remove leaves from stem
and steam or braise

CHAYOTE
(also called Buddha's Hand Gourd)
fat6 sau2 gwaa1

佛手瓜

also called hap6 zoeng2 gwaa1 合掌瓜
Season: May to October. How to eat:
Peel, cut in half, remove the seed and
roast, sauté, stir-fry or grate for a salad

CHESTNUT
leot6 zi2

栗子

also called fung1 leot6 風栗 and baan2
leot6 板栗
Season: All year
How to eat: Peel and roast, stir-fry or
boil (can be purchased already peeled)

CHINESE FLOWERING CABBAGE

coi1 sam1

菜芯

Season: All year
How to eat: Trim a slice off the end then steam or blanche

CHINESE KALE

(also called Chinese Broccoli)
gaai3 laan4

芥蘭

Season: All year
How to eat: Trim a slice off the end then steam or blanche

CHIVES - GREEN

gau2 coi1

韭菜

Season: All year
How to eat: Trim a slice off the ends,
thinly slice and add to stir-fries,
scrambled eggs or dumpling filling

CHIVES - YELLOW

gau2 wong4

韭黃

also called gau2 wong4 韭王
Season: All year
How to eat: Trim ends, cut into short
segments and add to soup, stir-fries or
salads

CORIANDER

(also called Cilantro) - jyun4 sai1

芫茜 also called jyun4 seoi1 芫荽
and hoeng1 seoi1 香荽
Season: All year
How to eat: Cut off roots and wash the
remaining stems and leaves then chop
and use as garnish or in salad

CUCUMBER

ceng1 gwaa1

青瓜
also called wong4 gwaa1 黃瓜
Season: All year
How to eat: Peel and slice

DAIKON
(also called White Radish)
baak6 lo4 baak6

白蘿蔔

Season: All year
How to eat: Peel and eat raw, roast, pickle or use in soup

EDAMAME
(also called Young Soybeans)
mou4 dau6

毛豆

Season: April to September
Boil for 15 minutes in water with a pinch of salt and a star anise, drain, cool, open the pods and eat the beans inside

ENOKI MUSHROOM
gam1 gu1

金菇

Season: All year
How to eat: Stir-fry, braise or add to soup

FLOWERING CHIVES
gau2 coi1 faa1

韭菜花

Season: All year
How to eat: trim off stem, cut into small segments and add to stir-fries, salads or scrambled eggs

GARLIC (SINGLE HEAD)
duk6 syun3

獨蒜

also called daai6 syun3 大蒜
When in season: All year
How to use: Peel and use like regular garlic

GARLIC STEMS
syun3 sam1

蒜芯

Season: All year
How to eat: Trim ends, chop into small segments and stir-fry

GINGER (NEW SEASON)

goeng1

薑

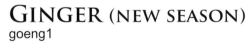

Season: New season from May to August; old ginger all year
How to eat: Peel away skin, chop, use in soup, add to stir-fries, braises or add to cup of hot water and drink

GREEN RADISH

ceng1 lo4 baak6

青蘿蔔

Season: May to October
How to eat: Peel and slice

HAIRY GOURD
mou4 gwaa1

毛瓜

also called zit3 gwaa1 節瓜
Season: April to August
How to eat: Peel, chop and stir-fry,
sauté or add to soup

JICAMA
(also called Yam Bean)
saa1 got3

沙葛

Season: All year
How to eat: Peel, slice and eat raw or
cut into matchsticks and stir-fry

Kudzu Root
got3 gan1

葛根

also called fan2 got3 粉葛
Season: All year
How to eat: Peel, cut into pieces and add to soup or stew

Lalang Grass Rhizome
maau4 gan1

茅根

Season: June to September
How to use: Make herbal tea infusion for medicinal use

LILY BULB
baak3 hap6

百合

Season: All year
How to eat: Add to soup, stir-fry or
blanch and add to salad

LONG BEANS
dau6 gok3

豆角

Season: All year
How to eat: Cut into segments and stir-
fry, sauté or steam

LOTUS ROOT
lin4 ngau5

蓮藕

Season: April to August
How to eat: Peel; sauté, stir-fry, blanche or steam

MUSTARD LEAVES
gaai3 coi3

芥菜

Season: All year
How to eat: Stir-fry or add to soup or salad

NIGHT FRAGRANT FLOWER
je6 hoeng1 faa1

夜香花

Season: June to July
How to eat: Add to scrambled eggs or soup

OLD YELLOW CUCUMBER
lou5 wong4 gwaa1

老黄瓜

Season: April to September
How to eat: Peel and slice

OYSTER MUSHROOMS (LEFT)

sau3 zan1 gu1

秀珍菇

Season: All year

How to eat: Slice and sauté, stir-fry, braise or add to soup

KING OYSTER MUSHROOMS (RIGHT)

hang6 baau6 gu1

杏鮑菇

Season: All year

How to eat: Slice and sauté, stir-fry, braise or add to soup

Pea Shoots
dau6 miu4

豆苗

Season: March to June
How to eat: Stir-fry or sauté

Pumpkin
naam4 gwaa1

南瓜

Season: All year
How to eat: Cut in half lengthwise, peel, remove seeds, chop and roast, steam, braise, sauté or stir-fry

SHALLOTS
cung1 tau4

蔥頭
Season: All year
How to eat: Peel off dried skin, slice
and use in sautéing & stir-frying

SHANGHAI BOK CHOY
soeng6 hoi2 baak6 coi3

上海白菜
also called siu2 tong4 coi3 小唐菜
Season: All year
How to eat: Trim stem, steam or braise
whole or slice and add to salad

Snow Peas
(also called Mange Tout)
ho4 laan4 dau6

荷蘭豆

Season: All year
How to eat: Remove stem then steam,
sauté, stir-fry or blanch

Spring Onion
(also called Scallion)
cung1

蔥

Season: All year
How to use: Cut off roots and slice both
white and green parts; add to stir-fries,
salads, soups

Straw Mushrooms
cou2 gu1

草菇

Season: All year
How to eat: Use whole or slice then sauté, stir-fry, braise or add to soup

Sugarcane
gam1 ze3

甘蔗

Season: June to September
How to eat: Peel off outer layer and chew stalk

SWEET POTATO
faan1 syu4

番薯

also called gam1 syu4 甘薯
and dei6 gwaa1 地瓜
Season: All year
How to eat: Peel, chop then roast, stir-fry, sauté or add to soup

SWEET POTATO LEAVES
faan1 syu4 jip6

番薯葉

also called dei6 gwaa1 jip6 地瓜葉
Season: June to September
How to eat: Trim stem and sauté or stir-fry

SWORD LETTUCE
jao4 mahk5 choi3

油麥菜

Season: All year
How to eat: Use in salads or stir-fry

TARO
wu6 tau4

芋頭

Season: All year
How to eat: Peel, chop and steam,
roast or boil

WATER CHESTNUT
maa5 tai2

馬蹄

Season: All year
How to eat: Peel then slice or dice
and use in stir-fries or dumpling filling;
Alternatively blanch and put in salads

WATERCRESS
sai1 joeng4 coi3

西洋菜

Season: All year
How to eat: Cut into segments and stir-
fry or add to soup or salads

WATER SPINACH
ung3 coi3

蕹菜 also called tung3 coi3 通菜
and hung1 sam1 coi3 空心菜
Season: May to September
How to eat: Trim slice off stem bottom
then cut stem into short segments
keeping leaves whole and sauté or stir-fry

WILD RICE SHOOT
(also called Water Bamboo Shoot)
gaau1 seon2

茭筍
Season: May to September
How to eat: Pull away outer layer of
stalk then slice and sauté or stir-fry

Winter Melon
(also called Wax Gourd)
dung1 gwaa1

冬瓜

When in season: All year
How to use: Peel, remove seeds, dice
and braise or add to soups

Winter Mushroom
(also called Fragrant Mushroom)
dung1 gu1

冬菇

also called hoeng1 gu1 香菇
Season: All year. How to eat: Trim bottom
of stem, leave whole or slice then braise,
stew, sauté or stir-fry

TOFU

豆腐

dau6 fu6

BEAN SPROUTS
ngaa4 coi3

芽菜

also called dau6 ngaa4 豆芽
How to use: Stir-fry

CLOTH WRAPPED TOFU
bou3 baau1 dau6 fu6

布包豆腐

How to use: Steam

FIRM TOFU

ngaang6 dau6 fu6

硬豆腐

How to use: Cube and stir-fry or braise

SOFT TOFU

baan2 dau6 fu6

板豆腐

How to use: Slice and add to soup

FRIED TOFU
dau6 paau3

豆泡

How to use: Use whole in braises; Slice and add to stir-fries; Stuff and steam

PIG'S BLOOD JELLY
zyu1 hung4

豬紅

How to use: Add to congee or soup

Pressed Tofu
dau6 gon1

豆乾

How to use: Add to stir-fries, salads or sandwiches (note: some have been flavoured with five-spice or other spices while others are plain)

FRESH SEAFOOD

海鮮

hoi2 sin1

ABALONE
baau6 jyu4

鮑魚

How to prepare: Steam or sauté

BROWN SCALLOP
daai3 zi2

帶子

How to prepare: Steam or sauté

GEODUCK CLAM

zoeng6 bat6 pong5

象拔蚌

How to prepare: Slice and sauté or add to soup

GOLDEN THREADFIN BREAM

hung4 saam1 jyu4

紅衫魚

How to prepare: Leave whole and steam, roast, braise, sauté or grill

GRASS CARP
waan5 jyu4

鯇魚
also called cou2 jyu4 草魚
How to prepare: Steam or add to soup

GROUPER
sek6 baan1 jyu4

石斑魚
How to prepare: Leave whole and
steam; Cut into segments and braise;
Slice and add to congee

HAIRTAIL
(also called Belt fish)
daai3 jyu4

帶魚

also called ngaa4 daai3 jyu4 牙帶魚
How to prepare: Cut into segments and
braise, sauté or grill

MANTIS PRAWN
laai6 niu6 haa1

瀨尿蝦

How to prepare: Leave in shell and
steam or boil

MULLET
wu1 jyu4

烏魚

How to prepare: Leave whole and
steam, roast or grill; Cut into segments
and add to soup

OYSTER
hou4

蠔

also called ho4 蚵
How to prepare: Add to soup, congee or
scrambled eggs

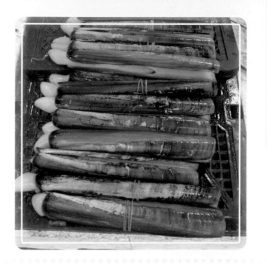

POMFRET
coeng1 jyu4

鯧魚
How to prepare: Leave whole and
sauté, braise, steam or grill

RAZOR CLAM
cing1 zi2

蟶子
How to prepare: Stir-fry or steam

SEA BREAM

lap6 jyu4

立魚

How to use: Leave whole and steam,
roast, sauté or grill

SILVER FISH

ngan4 jyu4

銀魚

also called baak6 faan6 jyu4 白飯魚
How to prepare: Steam or saute

Snakehead
saang1 jyu4

生魚

How to prepare: Leave whole and steam or slice through bone and use in soup

Squid
jau4 jyu4

魷魚

How to prepare: Remove quill and ink sack then slice or cut into pieces and stir-fry or sauté

TONGUE SOLE
taat3 saa1 jyu4

撻沙魚

How to prepare: Leave whole and steam, poach or braise

YELLOW CROAKER
wong4 faa1 jyu4

黃花魚

How to prepare: Leave whole and steam, braise or sauté

DRIED & OTHER FOODS

雜貨

zaap6 fo3

also called zaap6 fo3 什貨

APRICOT KERNELS
naam4 bak1 hang6

南北杏

How to use: Substitute for almonds

ARHAT FRUIT
lo4 hon3 gwo2

羅漢果

How to use: Break open, use as a sweetener or traditional medicine

AZUKI BEANS
hung4 dau6

紅豆

How to use: Cover with water, simmer until soft but still holding their shape; Alternatively use as congee or soup ingredient

BAMBOO LEAVES
zuk4 jip6

竹葉

How to use: Soak in warm water for 20 minutes then use as a wrapper to roast fish in or for *songzi* (the steamed parcel eaten during Dragon Boat Festival)

CABBAGE - DRIED
coi3 gon1

菜乾

How to use: Soak in water for 10 minutes, chop and add to soup or stir-fries

CASSIA BARK
gwai3 pei4

桂皮

also called juk6 gwai3 肉桂
How to use: Substitute for cinnamon sticks

CHINESE DATES
(also called Jujube)
zou2

How to use: Eat as is or add to soup

CHRYSANTHEMUM FLOWERS
guk1 faa1

菊花

How to use: Add to hot water to make chrysanthemum tea

Cloud Ear Mushroom

wan4 ji5

雲耳

How to use: Soak in lukewarm water 20 minutes, slice and add to stir-fry, soup or salad

Day Lily Buds - Dried

gam1 zam1 faa1

金針花

How to use: Soak in water for 30 minutes until soft, drain and add to soup or stir-fries.

FISH MAW
jyu4 tou5

魚肚

also called faa1 gaau1 花膠
How to use: Soak until soft and add to soups, braises

GINKGO NUTS
baak6 gwo2

白果

How to use: Crack open shell, soak in water and remove skin, drain then add to congee or soups; alternatively stir-fry with a little olive oil and salt

HAWTHORN
(also called Haw Fruit)
saan1 zaa1

山楂

How to use: Rinse and eat as is or add to hot water for medicinal tea

HEGEMONY FLOWER
(also called Dragon Fruit Flower)
baa3 wong6 faa1

霸王花

How to use: Soak in water for 20 minutes, drain, chop and add to soup

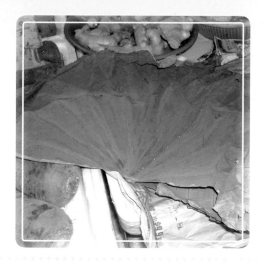

LOTUS LEAF
ho4 jip6

荷葉

How to use: Soak in water for 20 minutes then use as a wrapper to roast fish in

LOTUS SEED
lin4 zi2

蓮子

How to use: Soak in water 2 hours, drain then add to soup and congee

Mung Beans
luk6 dau6

綠豆

How to use: Rinse, cover with water, simmer until soft but they still hold their shape and use in salads; Alternatively add to congee or soup

Oyster - dried
hou4 si6

蠔豉

How to use: Add to congee or soak in warm water for 2 hours then add to soup

PRESERVED DUCK EGG
(also called Century Egg)
pei4 daan6

皮蛋

How to use: Add to congee

PRESERVED MUSTARD TUBER
zaa3 coi3

榨菜

How to use: Rinse, mince and add to stir-fries and steamed dishes

PRESERVED POTHERB MUSTARD
syut3 coi3

雪菜

How to use: Chop and add to noodle dishes or stir-fried pork or broad beans

PRESERVED VEGETABLE
mui4 coi3

梅菜

(two types: savoury, haam4 鹹; sweet, tim4 甜)

How to use: Rinse, soak in water for 30 minutes; chop into small pieces and add to braises, noodles or congee

Salted Egg
haam4 aap3 daan6

鹹鴨蛋

How to use: Add yolk to *songzi*, a glutinous rice dumpling wrapped in bamboo leaves traditionally eaten at Dragonboat Festival

Salted Horseradish
daai6 tau4 coi3

大頭菜

How to use: Add to stir-fries, braises, soups

SALTED MUSTARD VEGETABLE

haam4 syun1 coi3

鹹酸菜

How to use: Rinse, slice and add to braises, soups, noodle dishes and congee

SAUSAGE

laap1 coeng2

腊腸 (sometimes written 臘腸)
(yun2 coeng2 膶腸 includes liver)
How to use: Place on top of rice while it is steaming; use in fried rice

SCALLOPS – DRIED
(also called Conpoy)
jyun4 bui3

元貝 also called jiu4 cyu5 瑤柱
How to use: Soak in room-temperature water for 3 hours and add to soups or braises; or tear into strands and add to stir-fried rice

SEA CUCUMBER – DRIED
hoi2 sam1

海參
How to use: Soak in water 4 days (changing water each day) then chop and add to soups, braises or stir-fries

SHRIMP – DRIED
haa1 mai5

蝦米

How to use: Soak in room-temperature water for 20 minutes then add to stir-fries and soups

SNOW FUNGUS
syut3 ji5

雪耳

How to eat: Soak in room temperature water for 30 minutes or until soft, squeeze dry, cut in pieces and use in soup or braises

TANGERINE PEEL –
DRIED can4 pei4
陳皮
also called can4 gwat1 pei4 陳橘皮
How to use: Soak in warm water for 20 minutes, drain, slice into matchsticks and add to stews, braises or stir-fries; alternatively for medicinal use

TOFU SKIN SHEET –
DRIED
dau6 zuk1
腐竹
How to use: Soak in water until pliable then use as wrap for dim sum

Tofu Skin Stick – dried

zi1 zuk1

枝竹

How to use: Soak in water until pliable, cut into strips and stir-fry, braise or add to a salad

Winter Mushrooms – dried

dung1 gu1

冬菇

also called hoeng1 gu1 香菇
How to use: Rinse; soak in room temperature water for 1 hour; slice and use in soup, stir-fries, braises, etc

WOLFBERRY
(also called Goji Berries)
gau2 gei2 zi2

枸杞子

also called gei2 zi2 杞子
How to use: Add to soup or
chrysanthemum tea

WOOD EAR MUSHROOM
muk6 ji5
木耳
How to use: Soak in lukewarm water 20
minutes, slice and add to stir-fry, soup
or salad

ADDITIONAL VOCABULARY OF COMMONLY KNOWN FOODS

English	Romanization	Chinese
Apple	ping4 gwo2	蘋果
Apricot	hang6	杏
Asparagus	lou4 seon2	蘆筍
Banana	hoeng1 ziu1	香蕉
Broccoli	sai1 laan4 faa1	西蘭花
also called	ceng1 faa1 coi3	青花菜
Cabbage	je4 coi3	椰菜
Capsicum	dang1 lung4 ziu1	燈籠椒
Carrot	gam1 seon2	甘筍
also called	hung4 lo4 baak6	紅蘿蔔
Cashew	jiu1 gwo2	腰果
Celery	sai1 kan4	西芹
also called	kan4 coi3	芹菜
Cherry	ce1 lei4 zi2	車厘子
also called	jing1 tou4	櫻桃
Chilli	hung4 faan1 ziu1	紅番椒
also called	laat6 ziu1	辣椒
Clam	hin2	蜆

Crab	haai5	蟹
also called	pong4 haai5	螃蟹
Corn (maize)	suk1 mai5	粟米
also called	juk6 mai5	玉米
Courgette (zucchini)	ceoi3 juk6 gwaa1	翠玉瓜
Grape	tai4 zi2	提子
also called	pou4 tou4	葡萄
Kiwi fruit	kei4 ji6 gwo2	奇異果
also called	mei4 hau4 tou4	獼猴桃
Lemon	ning4 mung4	檸檬
Lime	ceng1 ning4	青檸
Lobster	lung4 haa1	龍蝦
Mandarin	gam1	柑
Onion	joeng4 cung1	洋蔥
Orange	caang4	橙
Peach	tou4 zi2	桃子
Peanut	faa1 sang1	花生
Pineapple	bo1 lo4	菠蘿

Pine nuts	cung4 zi2 jan4	松子仁
Plum	lei5 zai2	李仔
also called	bou3lam4	布林
Pomegranate	sek6 lau4	石榴
Potato	syu4 zai2	薯仔
Prawn (shrimp)	haa1	蝦
Soy milk	dau6 zoeng1	豆漿
Spinach	bo1 coi3	菠菜
Tangerine	gwat1	橘
Tomato	faan1 ke4	番茄

MARKET SIGNAGE

WEIGHTS

公斤
gung1 gan1
A kilogram

斤
gan1
A catty; approximately 600g.
Used only for vegetables. Signs
sometimes say 每斤 (mui5 gan1)
which means per catty.

磅
bong6
A pound, approximately 453g

兩
loeng2 (also written 两)
A tael; 37.5 grams (1/16th of a catty)

錢
cin4
A mace; 3.75g (1/10th of a tael)

克
hak1
A gram

WAYS FOOD IS SOLD

個
go3
means something is sold per piece, so:

8
元
一
個
means it costs HK$8 for one piece

份
fan6
means a portion, so:

7
元
份
means it costs HK$7 per portion

盆
pun4
means something is sold per bowl or basin, so:

5
元
盆
means it costs HK$5 per bowl

盒
hap6
means something is sold per small box or container, so:

9
元
盒
means it costs HK$9 per container

扎

zaat3 or zaap3
means a bunch or bundle, so:

2
元
扎　　means it costs HK$2 per
　　bunch

每

mui5
means each or per, so:

7
每
斤　　means it costs HK$7 per catty

Other measure words

| 條 | tiu4 | per piece (e.g. a single fish) |

包	baau1	a bag (e.g. garlic)
件	gin6	a piece (e.g. dried fish)
片	pin3	a slice (e.g. bread)
枝	zi1	a branch (e.g. sugarcane)
只	zek3	per piece (e.g. some seafood)
隻	zek3	per piece (e.g. crab)

Other signage used at the market

本地	bun2 dei6	locally grown
本港	bun2 gong2	from Hong Kong
新界	san1 gaai3	from the New Territories
中國	zung1 gwok3	from China
泰國	taai3 gwok3	from Thailand
日本	jat6 bun2	from Japan
美國	mei5 gwok3	from the USA
特級	dak6 kap1	special grade or type

CHINESE NUMBERS

1	一	jat1		20	二十	ji6 sap6
2	二	ji6		21	二十一	ji6 sap6 jat1
3	三	saam1		22	二十二	ji6 sap6 ji6
4	四	sei3		23	二十三	ji6 sap6 saam1
5	五	ng5		24	二十四	ji6 sap6 sei3
6	六	luk6		25	二十五	ji6 sap6 ng5
7	七	cat1		26	二十六	ji6 sap6 luk6
8	八	baat3		27	二十七	ji6 sap6 cat1
9	九	gau2		28	二十八	ji6 sap6 baat3
				29	二十九	ji6 sap6 gau2
10	十	sap6				
11	十一	sap6 jat1		30	三十	saam1 sap6
12	十二	sap6 ji6		31	三十一	saam1 sap6 jat1
13	十三	sap6 saam1		32	三十二	saam1 sap6 ji6
14	十四	sap6 sei3		33	三十三	saam1 sap6 saam1
15	十五	sap6 ng5		34	三十四	saam1 sap6 sei3
16	十六	sap6 luk6		35	三十五	saam1 sap6 ng5
17	十七	sap6 cat1		36	三十六	saam1 sap6 luk6
18	十八	sap6 baat3		37	三十七	saam1 sap6 cat1
19	十九	sap6 gau2		38	三十八	saam1 sap6 baat3

39	三十九	saam1 sap6 gau2
40	四十	sei3 sap6
41	四十一	sei3 sap6 jat1
42	四十二	sei3 sap6 ji6
43	四十三	sei3 sap6 saam1
44	四十四	sei3 sap6 sei3
45	四十五	sei3 sap6 ng5
46	四十六	sei3 sap6 luk6
47	四十七	sei3 sap6 cat1
48	四十八	sei3 sap6 baat3
49	四十九	sei3 sap6 gau2
50	五十	ng5 sap6
51	五十一	ng5 sap6 jat1
52	五十二	ng5 sap6 ji6
53	五十三	ng5 sap6 saam1
54	五十四	ng5 sap6 sei3
55	五十五	ng5 sap6 ng5
56	五十六	ng5 sap6 luk6

57	五十七	ng5 sap6 cat1
58	五十八	ng5 sap6 baat3
59	五十九	ng5 sap6 gau2
60	六十	luk6 sap6
61	六十一	luk6 sap6 jat1
62	六十二	luk6 sap6 ji6
63	六十三	luk6 sap6 saam1
64	六十四	luk6 sap6 sei3
65	六十五	luk6 sap6 ng5
66	六十六	luk6 sap6 luk6
67	六十七	luk6 sap6 cat1
68	六十八	luk6 sap6 baat3
69	六十九	luk6 sap6 gau2
70	七十	cat1 sap6
71	七十一	cat1 sap6 jat1
72	七十二	cat1 sap6 ji6
73	七十三	cat1 sap6 saam1
74	七十四	cat1 sap6 sei3

75	七十五	cat1 sap6 ng5
76	七十六	cat1 sap6 luk6
77	七十七	cat1 sap6 cat1
78	七十八	cat1 sap6 baat3
79	七十九	cat1 sap6 gau2
80	八十	baat3 sap6
81	八十一	baat3 sap6 jat1
82	八十二	baat3 sap6 ji6
83	八十三	baat3 sap6 saam1
84	八十四	baat3 sap6 sei3
85	八十五	baat3 sap6 ng5
86	八十六	baat3 sap6 luk6
87	八十七	baat3 sap6 cat1
88	八十八	baat3 sap6 baat3
89	八十九	baat3 sap6 gau2
90	九十	gau2 sap6
91	九十一	gau2 sap6 jat1
92	九十二	gau2 sap6 ji6
93	九十三	gau2 sap6 saam1
94	九十四	gau2 sap6 sei3
95	九十五	gau2 sap6 ng5
96	九十六	gau2 sap6 luk6
97	九十七	gau2 sap6 cat1
98	九十八	gau2 sap6 baat3
99	九十九	gau2 sap6 gau2
100	一百	jat1 baak3

10 HONG KONG FOOD MARKETS

NORTH POINT'S MARKETS

North Point has two excellent markets. One is on Chun Yeung Street between North Point Road and Tong Shui Road at the terminus of the North Point tram. The second, the Java Road Market, is the multi-storey building on the corner of Tong Shui Road and Java Road to the north and east of Chun Yeung Street. Seafood, meat and dried food are on the ground floor and an excellent range of fruit, vegetables and tofu are sold one floor up. Don't miss the restaurant stalls on the market's top floor.

Directions: Take the tram to the North Point terminus or alight at the North Point Road stop on King's Road and walk one block north (towards the water) to Chun Yeung Street. From the North Point MTR exit A1 turn left and cross Shu Kuk Street. Turn right and cross Java Road then turn left and continue walking one block to Java Road Market.

BOWRINGTON ROAD MARKET

Bowrington Road Market operates on the street along the intersection of Bowrington Road and the eastern end of Wanchai Road. The market bustles with activity and friendly vendors selling fish, meat, fruit and vegetables.

Directions: 1) Take the tram along Johnston Road to the Canal Road stop. Walk south (away from the water) across Johnston Road. Turn right and walk a short block to Bowrington Road and turn left.

2) From the Causeway Bay MTR exit B, cross Johnston Road and turn right. Walk along Johnston Road. After you pass under the Canal Road Bridge/flyover walk another short block to Bowrington Road and turn left.

WANCHAI MARKET

Wanchai Market sprawls around the area of Stone Nullah Lane, Cross Street and Wanchai Road. Stalls sell fish, seafood, meat, noodles, tofu, fruit, vegetables, *bauzi* (steamed buns) and traditional cakes. The Wanchai Market building on Queen's Road East houses more vendors offering seafood, meat, vegetables, fruit and tofu but lacks the bustle of the street stalls.

Directions: From the tram stop in front of the Wanchai MTR station's exit A3, walk across Johnston Road (away from the MTR station) and turn left. Walk a few steps and turn right on Stone Nullah Lane.

SHAU KEI WAN MARKET

Shau Kei Wan's lively street market offers a wide choice of excellent seafood, vegetables, fruit, noodles and dried foods. The main area of activity is around Kam Wa Street.

Directions: From Shau Kei Wan MTR exit C turn left. Stalls begin a few steps ahead. The first junction is Kam Wa Street. Turn right and cross the street.

GRAHAM STREET MARKET

The Graham Street Market has been under threat of closure for some time but until that actually happens the market offers a prime location to shop for fresh vegetables, fruit, dried goods, noodles and tofu. The seafood selection is smaller than at other markets.

Directions: Graham Street is within walking distance from anywhere in Central. The market runs between Queen's Road Central and Lyndhurst Terrace.

ABERDEEN MARKET

Vendors are so closely packed into the Aberdeen Market that there's hardly room for customers to wiggle their way through. The market's highlight is the ultra-fresh seafood, not surprising given that the Aberdeen Wholesale Fish Market is around the corner. Fruit and vegetables are also excellent.

Directions: From behind Aberdeen's main bus terminus on Aberdeen Praya Road, walk away from the water along

Tung Sing Road to Wu Pak Street. Turn left and walk one block to Cheng Tu Road. Turn right and walk straight ahead until just past Nam Ning Street. The market is on the lower storey of the Aberdeen Municipal Services Building on the opposite side of the street.

Mongkok Market

Mongkok Market runs along Canton Road between Mongkok Road and Shantung Street. The stalls sell beautiful fruit and vegetables at considerably cheaper prices than on Hong Kong Island as well as meat, seafood, fish balls and cakes, dried goods and medicinal plants.

Directions: From Exit A2 at the Mongkok MTR station, walk west along

Fife Street crossing Portland Street, Shanghai Street, Reclamation Street and one further block to Canal Road.

Yau Ma Tei Market

Yau Ma Tei Market operates along Reclamation Street between Gansu Street and Nanking Street. The Yau Ma Tei Market building on the corner of Gansu and Reclamation Streets houses a few seafood and vegetable vendors on the ground floor. Similar to the Mongkok Market, this market offers fruit, vegetables, meat, seafood, dried goods and medicinal plants.

Directions: From Exit A at the Jordan MTR station, walk west along Jordan Road crossing Parkes Street, Woosung Street, Temple Street and Shanghai

Street. Turn right on Shanghai Street and walk one block to Nanking Street. Turn left and walk one block to Reclamation Street.

TAI PO MARKET

Tai Po Market is located in the town of Tai Po in the New Territories. It is one of Hong Kong's best markets and well worth the trek. The seafood on the ground floor is one of the freshest selections in Hong Kong. Fruit, vegetables and dry goods are on the next floor up and the top floor houses a lively food court packed with stalls selling delicious noodles, congee, dim-sum and more.

Directions: Take the MTR to Tai Po Market station. From the turnstiles turn right and walk straight. Follow the covered walkway around the curve to the right and under the rail tracks. The market is the three-storey building on the opposite side of the street.

CHEUNG CHAU MARKET

The highlight of Cheung Chau's market is the seafood which arrives ultra-fresh from the boats moored next to the market. Seafood and meat are on the ground floor with more seafood, vegetables and fruit on the first floor.

Directions: From Pier 5 at the Central Ferry Terminals, take the ferry to Cheung Chau. As you leave Cheung Chau's Ferry Terminal turn right and walk straight until you come to the Cheung Chau Municipal Services Building.

ORGANIC MARKETS

For anyone wanting to purchase organic produce, the Organic Farmers' Market at the Central Star Ferry Pier is held Sundays from 11am to 5pm.

Kadoorie Farm and Botanic Garden (Lam Kam Road, Tai Po, New Territories; www.kfbg.org) holds an organic farmers mini-market on the first Sunday of the month from 9:30am to 5pm.
Directions: From either Tai Po or Tai Wo MTR East Rail Stations, take bus 64K and alight at Kadoorie Farm.

Lion's Nature Education Centre (Hiram's Highway, Sai Kung, New Territories) holds an organic farmers market on Sundays from 9:30am to 4pm.
Directions: From Choi Hung MTR station take Public Light Bus 1A from Exit C2 or Kowloon Motor Bus 92 from Exit B. Alight at Pak Kong, opposite the Centre's entrance.

Acknowledgements

I want to thank the many patient market vendors who took time to help me understand the names of various foods and how to cook them.

In addition, two online Cantonese dictionaries helped me tremendously in my research. The first is the Chinese University's website, http://arts.cuhk.edu.hk/Lexis/lexi-can, and the second is www.cantonese.sheik.co.uk. I have used the Jyutping romanisation of the Cantonese.

Pronunciation

This very brief guide is adapted from cantonese.sheik.co.uk, with thanks.

Letters at the start of words
c – only appears at the start of a word and is always pronouced 'ch'. Note it is not a strong 'ch' sound; the emphasis is slightly on a 't' sound.
j – at the start of the word, this should be pronounced 'y'. An example is 'ji' (two), which is prononuced 'yee'.
ng – similar to the 'gn' in 'gnaw'.
z – this may be treated as a 'j' like in 'jam' but it is more like a cross between a 'j' and a 'z'.

Vowels within words
u – like the 'oo' in 'moon'.
a – like the 'u' in 'cup'.
aa – like the 'ar' in 'farm'.
i – like the 'ee' in 'see'.

Vowels at the end of words

i – as above, like the English 'see'.
u – as above, it retains its 'oo' sound, e.g. 'jyu' (fish) sounds like 'you'.
o – like the English 'oar', e.g. 'do' (many) would be pronounced like 'door'.
aa – like the 'ar' in 'farm'.
eoi – a soft sound that doesn't occur in English. The closest would be the 'oy' sound in 'boy' but the emphasis is more on a 'u' sound than an 'o'. This is a common sound in Cantonese, e.g. 'seoi' (water).
au – like the 'ow' in 'how' or 'now'.
e – like the English 'air', e.g. 'ce' is pronounced like the English 'chair'.
ei – like the 'ay' in 'hay' or 'may'.
ou – like the English 'oh', e.g. 'mou' is pronounced like the English 'mow'.

Tones

Like other Chinese languages, Cantonese is tonal. This means that many similar-sounding words have different meanings depending on which tone is used. The Jyutping romanisation uses six numbers to represent the tones. They are:

Tone 1: high level flat (or falling)
Tone 2: rising to high level
Tone 3: mid level flat
Tone 4: low level falling
Tone 5: rising to mid level
Tone 6: low level flat

Low, mid and high represent the tonal range of each speaker. So, speak tone 6 words as deep as you can while still sounding natural. Tone 3 words should be spoken in your normal voice and tone 1 words should be higher.

It will take time to get the hang of this, but markets are a good place to practise!

ABOUT THE AUTHOR

After receiving formal training at Pru Leith's in London, Pam Shookman worked in a number of London restaurants and ran the test kitchen for Eric Treuille at Books for Cooks in Notting Hill. She spent many years living and eating across east Asia, including periods in Malaysia, Indonesia, Vietnam, China and Hong Kong. She was Food Editor for *Time Out Beijing*, contributed to *Slow Food* and *The Insider's Guide to Beijing* and ran cooking classes.

As this book was going to press Pam Shookman was diagnosed with cancer from which she subsequently died in London. She was passionate about helping people to cook and to use fresh local ingredients. She enjoyed high-end dining but it was street food, in all its quirky local manifestations, that really excited her. This book is a reflection of that commitment to the fresh and the local. She intended that it should be of practical use, carried into markets, becoming stained and dog-eared in the process.

The publication of this book following her death is due in no small measure to the enthusiastic support of Tony Tan, author of *Tony Tan's Hong Kong*, and her husband, Peter Wood.